Five Red Sentries

Five Red Sentries

Raye Hendrickson

thistledown press

Thistledown Press Ltd.
410 2nd Ave. North
Saskatoon, Saskatchewan, S7K 2C3
www.thistledownpress.com

Library and Archives Canada Cataloguing in Publication

Title: Five red sentries / Raye Hendrickson.
Names: Hendrickson, Lydia, 1956- author.
Description: Poems.
Identifiers: Canadiana 20190063289 | ISBN 9781771871952 (softcover)
Classification: LCC PS8615.E5335 F58 2019 | DDC C811/.6—dc23

Cover and book design by Jackie Forrie
Author photo by Kathryn Hamre
Printed and bound in Canada

Thistledown Press gratefully acknowledges the financial support of the Canada Council for the Arts, the Saskatchewan Arts Board, and the Government of Canada for its publishing program.

CONTENTS

If Only I Knew My Part So Well

take a section of orange
hang it in the sky
you have the moon
where the slice pales
juice barely tinting the thin core
the night almost
glinting through tight-stretched skin

can you see through me
more clearly
in the dark?

its curve a comma punctuating
the black page
or the agogic mark for singing
cueing stars to linger
over the first
note of a phrase

daybreak: eclipsed, the crescent waxes
in the wings behind light

Acrobat

Springboarding from the edge of the earth
I wrap my palm
around the waxing
moon.

Riding a swing
higher and higher
I backflip
into the crescent's hollow.
Moon shards, flaky and friable
needle me to sleep.

Polaris in my eyes, I measure
the distance to the Dipper's corner.
This time, tightroping.

Attentive Image

after an oil painting by Arthur F. McKay

This circle wants to spin me
spit me from the centre
where I float
tumbling head over head
over feet flailing
never fixing a grip
never rooted in
spinning
throws me
into a cavity
radial arm centrifugal
force I spill its length roll into the border.

Motion slows. Textures — in the centre, chaos, joy
beyond this corridor, black security ring   then crumpled
backdrop   then edges
of nothing: absurdity not even infinity

reality
the spin

Why I Want to Travel the Stars

Because night wears belly rings
and stars are not ashamed.
Diamonds sear skin.

I want to hear night singing
smell night blooming
see night birthing.

Because stars call me by name, and I have a name
for the star five to the left of Polaris.

I want to see the roots of a star
look down the throat of a star
fall through a star to the other side
of my questions about God
touch a star and burn away the lump in my throat
carry home a piece of red.

Time is languid among the stars.
Light is too slow, warp drives and slip
streams are still science fiction. But
communication doesn't need speech, because
particles light years apart
change spins simultaneously.

Because tectonic ruptures fray the cord
between mantle and cosmos
and earth is crying.
Stars tire from burning, but heat forges strength.

Because our wings were clipped at birth.

Fragments from Hubble

Suns brighter than the star in the east are caught
burning, announcing

salvations. Interstellar abstracts
steal my breath, splash outrageous greens, plums
and magentas, twist, swirl. Surely
dreams are the skin of nebular clouds
pink and fleshy, veiny.

Dense galaxies crowd the universe. In the dark
there are spirals so dazzling
I never want to walk a straight line again.

When you kiss me, it is the bone
of stars colliding, releasing something new.

ReVision

Every other time I faced the locked door I turned
away. Shaking knees, nausea. This time
I fit the key, then stumble through

to a new dream. In my hands a rainbow
sizzling, sparking. The colours split
converge   begin to spin, fast
and faster
a vortex
of white
light   I am
caught   sucked in
skin
peels   the thread
holding
me
snaps.

Dancing alone, the blue arc whirls so fast
sky thinks itself a circle. Umber, russet, gold, taupe.
Lavender, pink, orange, red, magenta, turquoise, emerald, terra cotta.
The arc slows.
Stops.
Dizzy, it wraps
its arms around earth.

My fingers stretch
to touch its skin.
Sky's belly slides
away, and sapphire drips down my arm.

Don't ever tell me that dismantled nights
have nothing to do with emptied eyes.
To understand all this
stillness is to believe that black holes
are only momentary patches of chaos
the spinning of skulls so full
everything seems dark.

Isosceles

Consider this triangle, so certain
so definite:

angle up, angle down, horizon along the bottom
so smooth, so steep.

I want to climb one side
and when I reach the peak

perhaps I'll stay forever
teetering.

Or return
to the same plane but not time

a place I've already been
water curving me like skin.

Silver

The argentine night
silvering the tongue
tastes of other worlds
you can cry over.

Water's sheen
feeds my gut more
than any coin.
I am hungry to press my palm
into a dolphin's silver skin.

The Other End of Motion

Water gets itchy unless it flows; fine
abrasive sand scrubs driftwood
from its belly. Water wriggles
and writhes, obeys the rhythm from far
dances dirty, dances tide.

The moon is the other end:
wane wax ebb flow recede advance drain fill sap
energize deplete animate
see how it brings me to shore, splashes
waterblood, flirts
with trinity: wings, womb, web.

The Curiosity of Water

To be drawn up a pipe
bloat just enough, then free-fall
a lone drip, to the cold, metal sink; how does it feel

to be that sheet of rain
caught in wind's grip, driven
against a windowpane and scattered;

to be wave after wave
white spew in a storm
all the tumbling?

What if I am slowed
by cold to stillness, trapped
frozen, unable to breathe?

Or heated to a frenzy
poured over leaves, infused until
I am other?

The sting when a stone skips
across my skin, the compulsion
to ripple from the impact.

Here's how it feels to find a crack. I will push
flow, or simply sit until I gain entry.
Time is on my side.

It's infinitely satisfying to somersault
from the clouds, ride the air
land softly

dribble down her sweet Scottish neck
between collar and skin
travel her spine.

I Don't Remember

the last call of the sirens
that aching chord reverberating off canyon walls
a peal echoing from a bell tower.
My gaze is urgent, to will my body over the edge
of the boat or the back of the world.
I fight to wrap my red striped scarf around my ears
cocoon myself.

The steep whitecap roller coaster hurls
my craft to the side of the gorge
traps me in a crevice as narrow
as the path of a snail.
I don't remember toiling to free myself
losing my balance   knowing I am lost.

I remember icy water
the blackness of sinking
silence
safety
of the deep.

Silence as Curriculum

Stuck in the middle
of open space somewhere
— William Robertson, "Father" from
Standing on My Own Two Feet

When space ships blow up, vacuum swallows
the bang; sounds are added for science fiction fans.
But what if the loss of lives was silent, witnessed
just with our eyes, our bellies?

Alone on a calm day, the prairie
drives blood to my fingers.
Every cell quickens. Then,
then: my shoulders drop, my jaw
falls to neutral, my feet root, my brain unclenches.

It's not such a bad thing, this
endless sight line, not even
a distant tree for texture. My bones
are open to the sky, marrow fed by blue.
The prairie is fiber, complex food. I am sated.

Eat silence for lunch, take a lifetime to digest.

To the Dunes

A beetle scuttles over cypress roots
black carapace bouncing light
into my eyes, escapes the sun's rays.
Heat swirls around my hatless head. It's getting hotter
and sweat drips down my back.
Around the next bend

the sand dunes. Waves folded
over and over in an arid ocean.
I am surprised by the prairie sunflowers
the reed grasses spinning
circles in the sand.

How else can joy be worn?
I throw off my clothes
lie down.
Nothing
between me and earth.

Birds Blown Sideways, Qu'Appelle Valley

The lake in full ruff summons me with white-cap passion.
Clouds skim into sculpture: eagle
becomes horse, becomes antler, giant, cathedral.

The wind is a solid today, my journey to the shore
like wading through treacle.
Sand thrashes the water, I wrestle with my hood
turn my back to the gale, lean hard.

Sand pelts my body, fills the sky.

I find shelter in a patch of dried wire rush
burrow down. The world
is a strip of dust-laden reeds
rustling like pick-up-sticks
and the wind — a roaring avalanche, waterfall thunder.

In my abdomen, a quivering
my cells in collective quickstep.

Flax

No other crop will be the prairie ocean
both oil and cloth.
Flax cracks its jaw and smacks its lips as it tracks
grasshoppers waxing their legs. If *f* gets lost
all you have is lax, a day without colour; and Flax
knows that days like that aren't really about blue.
So Flax never stops its imitation of sky and water.
What could be better than to see everything?

Werifesteria

from the Old English

forgotten country roads
that meander to nowhere
to everywhere I want to be

the inside of a rainbow, where colour
laughs at the storm that lost its teeth:
shredded clouds   fizzled lightning

a peeled grape, flesh still holding shape
translucent, exposed like new snake
slippery on my tongue

the vein of a willow leaf, long and sleek
conduit for nutrients and water
a channel for tears

all count, when I wander
longingly through the forest
in search of mystery

Track

Split jumps are my dream.
Walking the track
the railway track, I
balance, one foot
in front of the other:
spread-armed to catch myself from
falling, banging my shin.
But it's only two inches wide, and gymnasts
have four. This balance beam
has spikes that could pin me down.

Rail ties are the splint between sky and gravel
questions about green or stars and skinned knees.

Why I Carry Stones to the River

Because water needs obstacles
and this is the way it grows
leaves adolescence behind
finds its true mettle.

Because the solution to the problem
may come from these stones I carry.

Hard needs a sculptor, and
stones get thirsty as they work
to stitch the planet together.

Stones converse with other stones.
Water wants an offering to carry
to the other side of the world.
Stones rattle in my brain.

I can't tell if God is real or if
I should reveal one more layer
of truth about myself. I skip
wishes across water, and wishes are
most potent when flying. Life is lonely.
Rivulets stream around internal scar tissue
keeping it semi-pliable.

Life is lonely.

I dip my toes in water
to hold the ribbon of life
know that we will meet
and discover the full
measure of our desire.

Because I have taken stones away from the river.

The Hunt

Wings spread from sky to sky
hawk circles   catches an updraft   rises.
Then down, sweeping hard, turning sharply
around a cloud. Priming speed, accuracy.

Hawk's blood surges. One more
stretched arc, a steep bend toward the city.
Suburbs, strip malls, green spaces, destination downtown.
There: hawk crashes through the third floor window
sinks talons into the shallow-breathing woman
carries her life-force
up, away.

The woman's daughter finds her body
in the condo on the corner of College and Rose
at 11:27 AM when she comes to prepare lunch.

A Momentary Gap

My focus slips and she fades out
her words thin tissue barely stirring air
breathing that does not reach my ear.

When you add them up
gaps like these rend great holes
threaten the fabric where lives join.
Moths consuming memory.

Regret

Here's a page, a blank
page, my mind when faced with conflict.
I cannot find words, cannot
speak to refute to explain to defend to reconcile.
I just freeze strangled
by fear by the cold in my face my hair my gut and so
I hurt more.
And stare across the wide chasm . . . long
for the closeness that was.

The Beast

Grief prowls, stalks
waits for that moment
when you remember life will never be the same.
The sound of Eric's voice
the way he walks, swigs beer, dons his hat.
It takes my breath away
and tears snag
my eyes, clog my throat.
I don't have to turn my head very far
to see the beast slinking
behind me, just.

Lament

Once, I heard secrets
told to me by trees.
The windbreaks on my family farm spoke
of my father planting a blue spruce
at my brother's birth
a weeping birch at my sister's. Two siblings
tall and strong.

The trees whispered my father's love
how he planted and tended the crops, stood
in the field listening to the wheat grow.
Ate saskatoons from the bush along the railway track
as he read the sky. Harvested until after midnight.

My playground, sheltered by this circle of trees:
a row of granaries, a gas pump, my sibling trees
a tumble-down shed housing all the rusty
    nails, scraps of metal, and old golf clubs
    my father swore he would use some day.

But the windbreaks no longer speak, razed
with everything for a few acres of crop.
Everything but the granaries, five red sentries.
I stand in their shadow and the wind howls.

Nightwatch

Snapping cards and laughter, plaiting smoke
intermittent curses.

Cold linoleum bites
through pyjamas.
The silent watcher, dizzy
spies through the flue open to the kitchen below.

Mother frowns ceiling-ward.

Cramped muscles protest
as the should-be sleeper
crawls chastened
between now-icy sheets.
She strains to hear scores
tallied, her father shuffling

cards like rippling sand.

Burning Stubble

My father is on his way back to the harvested field
to offer incense to the weather god:
smoke, acrid perfume.
Can I come, too? I beg.

Flames crackle
      spit
snap
   surge
skyward. The heat sears my cheek.
A fist-sized ember arcs
to my feet, splits, disintegrates. I jump
back, hide behind my father.

Come on, he urges. *If you're careful you won't get hurt.*
I creep out again, hand raised, unable
to stop smoke snaking into my lungs.
I tighten my grip on the pitchfork, stalk
the edge of the burning pile. Wrench another fiery
bunch to the ground, spread its dying.

Window

this place
this village of Aylsham
splits my bounded
city soul

the sun pours in

I remember
biking to the farm, wind distorting my cheeks
hearing Mom call me in to supper
tight-roping the railway track
wanting Johnny to be the one to find me
on those hide-and-seek nights

this day is a window
an illumination
I hunt for
a piece of myself
that child who knew abandon

Markers

The granite slab names
my father perpetually in stone.

But he takes on flesh again:
A whiff of burning stubble, and I see him
        firing one straw pile after another
        until the whole field is aflame,
        staining the sink, the towels black with soot.
When I pass a golf course, he's the sole left-hander
        his drive casual and sure.
Crossword puzzles, cryptograms, *Reader's Digest*
        triple-story hardcovers.

The real mystery this: ten years absent
his broad hands and platter-sized fingernails
are as tangible as his etched date of death.

Schottische

You are eighty-one today, Mom
and here are fragments you've told me.
        You and your childhood friend Iva inseparable:
my left foot she called you, as you bore her weight;
her polio walking stick as she shuffled to the store, to shows.
        After grade eight, you became a Girl Friday
for the Pattersons, waxing their linoleum, running
errands and cooking eggs to earn money
safe from your father's gambling hands.
        You shadowed your brother to the dance hall
where he partnered with a broom
(too shy to ask girls) and swept around the floor.
Saving the schottische for you;
                                together you flew
everyone else straggling as the band's tempo quickened your feet.
Later, this same brother stumbled home
from the war. In the hospital you watched him shed
his hair, then his memory of you. Tears barely dry
    from this death, you laughed off teasing
about *that big Swede* with, *why would I ever marry* him?
All the while his ring under your glove.

Here are other fragments, my own pictures:
        That time you planted seedlings along the back lane
so Mrs. B. can't see us. Oh, our laughter! It took years
for the trees to grow tall, and by then Mrs. B. was gone.
        Home from school, I'd find you polishing
the hardwood floor, or ironing frost-dried sheets.
        Rolling out pastry for another fowl supper.

Rushing to the fields at harvest, roast beef and potatoes
steaming in the tea-towelled cardboard box.

Putting in the table leafs for company at Christmas.

Now, as your backbones crumble, you sweep
the silent kitchen, watch *Days of Our Lives*
hire a neighbour to wash your walls. I lean
against my living room doorway
keep in touch with phone calls, will never
know all of you.

Home for Thanksgiving

Though cars still line up outside
the pub, the post office
my childhood home
is a commercial ghost town.

Like a custom-sized coat
this three-by-ragged-two block village
fit me once.

Tonight, I walk its streets
and can't breathe.

In the Scheme of Things

It wasn't so big, just
an uncle trapping me in
the telephone alcove. His paw
on my teenage breast, his
whispers. My silence and feeling
soiled by more than the dirty
mark he left on my
white sweatshirt.

And it was just a drunk cousin
pinning me in the kitchen with
his foul words breathed
into my face: *You'd be pretty if*
you lost weight. My silence and
feeling ugly in spite of my Christmas
party clothes.

It was years before I could love my body, before
I believed someone would desire me.
A high price, in the scheme.

Grievance

Once you wore space as a great overcoat.
Age and illness stole
your flesh
then earth swallowed you whole.

Those bones
papered in skin

time-powdered.

Years later, this anger.
You sat at your desk for hours Dad
tracking numbers, balancing
the books. But my life's ledger
is found wanting — I feel cheated
of your time, your interest.

Your love slices deep.

Winter

Death plucks my mother
leaves me razed, orphaned.

I am the iced prairie.

I am the iced prairie bleak and white-shrouded.
I am unending iced prairie.

Cut Loose

floating, I am floating
feet churning for purchase

my soul no longer tethered
no longer daughtered

umbilical flapping without root
I am flying without licence

Peonies

Turning over in sleep one Thanksgiving weekend
my mother broke her hip.
It healed, but she broke the other one a few years later
in Arizona, driving her scooter off the curb: osteoporosis.

Her life an omnipresent oxygen nose ring
a four-wheeled walker, transient ischemic attacks.
She named words starting with *m, d, p,* or *g* to keep her mind
sharp, played Skip-Bo and rummy
as long as she could sit comfortably at the table. Drank wine
because she could.

Unregulated levels of potassium: short of breath
and dizzy in her hospital bed
she spoke of reunions, eager to join her long-dead husband.
A few hours after I left her side to join my sister for Christmas Eve
our mother shed her life.

∾∾∾

I return now to the weeded-over driveway
of her old corner lot on Main Street in Aylsham.
The mobile home, aluminum shed, garbage stand and bins
are gone.   The only proof
this space was inhabited is a ragged row of peonies
transplants from the downsizing move across town. One flower
is just past prime, its petals back-curled and brown-edged.

Its song catches my breath.

Graveside

Six months after burying my mother
in obstinate December ground
I return.

Perhaps I am trying not to think.
Perhaps I am steeling myself against to-be-expected pain;
perhaps, I am simply feeling strong.

But I am unprepared for the wreaths.

Stark white, red and green artificial flowers nestle
against rusty cedar boughs, and yellowed white roses
release still-lingering fragrance.

I finger dead foliage
the first child to return
to dispose of these remnants

unprepared for the impact
of my parents' fully occupied
double plot.

I pull a few dandelions
the yellow flowers my mother cursed
and quack grass, the choking weed.

What Is Left

These granaries: five red sentries
blaze against prairie-blue
burn after-images into canola

playing on that old harrow and the broken-down plough
both abandoned in the windbreak
red seeps into the earth
stories of my past:
trying to drive the red half-ton, clumsy
feet not getting the clutch right;
hitching a ride in the combine, a few
circuits around the field, just for fun;
picking raspberries, licking sticky fingers;
steering the little red tractor around the yard, wind in my face;
lining up tobacco tins by colour on the shelf
in the tumble-down shed;
counting the old golf clubs in the rafters.

The red mingles with sap
from my brother's fallen spruce
my sister's toppled birch, and the soil
is pierced.

Losing God

Absence is none of the following:
dissipating smoke, fading light
sun-dried fog. My neighbour's lasagne
seeping through the vent.
Snow melting, holes in wool socks.

Absence is half-formed prayers
rap for hymnody, borders without surety.
My entreaties fall into silence
and I walk on ice not bedrock.
My way in the world is tattered
as my once-theology.
I am stranger inside my skin.

When It All Began

On February 14, 2008, I swung
the hammer, hit the rock
you gave me. The geode
fell open, quartz flakes spilling
onto the counter.   What
a centre! Blues and purples, their crystal
edges sparking, exposed
like me bare before you.

You rock, you tell me, and I'm split
open, beginning to treasure myself
about to speak all the words
I keep inside because
they are boring, or not enough, or too scary.
Those hidden corners.

I left later that night, and
we'll never agree
as to who
kissed who first.

Influence

It's the moon, they say.
Makes some people crazy.
Like the time Lawrence jumped
off the bridge, thought he was flying
and no drugs in his system.
Energies on the flow like oceans
dragged over sand
by moon-pull, impulse.

Black-canvas infinity crisp-cut
by silver dollar moon.
Buildings and trees fall away.
I am night-winged into eternity.
But then, I have night vision
because of the moon.
Otherwise I would never see light
in the darkness.

Finding My Home

We've come home through a monsoon-like storm to find
our freshly dug trench for weeping
tile full. A moat, because the clay is gone. And no electricity
in the house. My whole body tenses
my muscles go rigid. My belly is so tight I can barely breathe.
I feel ready to fly apart from strain.

Elspeth braves the weather again to seek help
from our son-in-law. He comes, and in candlelight
assembles the sump pump, digs out the pit for the basin
and leaves. Then we wait for the return of power. When lights
come back on we hear the pump and rush downstairs to see water
drain away. But the lights flicker, go out again. Elspeth
goes for the candles we left upstairs.

In the dark, alone
in the corner of the basement
I feel the earth beneath my feet.
The concrete is gone, radon rock covers
most of the floor, but in this spot, it's just earth.
My earth. The soil upon which this house has rested
for ninety-one years. As I press my feet into the ground
my belly loosens. My breath is deep.

Just Beyond Reach

If I turn very quickly
I can just catch her moving.
— Kathleen Wall, "Landscapes With Absent Figure" from
Time's Body

Insubstantial ghost
pale face, pale dress, pale hair.

She comes to me in dreams, in the theatre
as I take my seat, in the hallways of friends.
Whispers to me, always so softly
I can hardly understand.

She arrives unannounced, taunts me always
just at the edge of sight. In her hand
a sheaf of papers with words the shape of poems.
She beckons, then fades away as soon as
I stretch out my hand.

In her wake
the scent of abundance.

Debra

We get the call Saturday morning. *If you want to see Deb*
you better come today, not tomorrow. It's that bad?
We thought we were going to tell tales, listen
to women's music. But Debra is unconscious
in her recliner, surrounded by family and friends.
We land in a vigil.
I feel awkward, stifle the impulse to run. What to say
to a friend whose partner is so near death?
To Deb's brother, sister, cousin, all of whom
I am only now meeting?   Chitchat, a tiny
conversation here, another there, stories about Deb;
the chairs around her always full, people shifting
switching, moving in and out.   Memories shared
of other deaths. Some people leave, others come.

Debra's breath is raspy, sort of wet. There is space
between some of her breaths, her apnea disturbing
the rhythm every now and then. *A terrible form*
of torture, her partner says. Because, is this particular
space the permanent one? But no, here is another
breath.   And another.   And we all wait for the last.

Then another space, the longest yet. All ears strain to hear
the next breath, not wanting to miss it. Finally
someone says, *She's gone.*   Just like that, the passage
from life to death.
So little separating us from her. And yet everything.

Time will bring grief, the awareness of her absence.
But for now we are all bound in this holy moment.

Two Circles

Precision stamps her mark: one perfect circle
with a thick, crisp edge, its imprint exactly even.
The centre of her circle is bare.
She leaves no shadows.

I slip into Creativity,
Precision's lover. Her circle offers
colours so vivid they squeeze my breath, textures
so diverse my skin tingles. In one sector, there are blank
canvases surrounded by ink pots labelled *earnest,*
expectant, burning, intense, do-or-die. I laugh
choose an easel; no paint-by-number template here.
Shall I dip my brush first into the jar of pebbly
or silky? Giggle or guffaw? Demure or brazen? Here's
what I will do: I'll splash maroon against
Precision's ring, blur her stamp. Dare her
to leave the mess, let Creativity catch
her hand and draw her into tango.

The Event Horizon

for Sharon

My Dad died last night, she said.
Those cracks in the drywall, never so distinct
the cosmos splintering. Again.
I revisit the emptiness
my own news eleven years ago.
He was alone. Her voice, bleak as a rain-grey day.
My sister found him this morning.

> Black hole. Separation.
> Death's gravity has sucked
> our fathers away. Beyond the point
> of no return. For a time
> we travel close, so close
> to the event horizon.

Her father's casket is draped
with his birthday quilt
family handprints stitched into the squares.

> Grief's trajectory gradually bends away.

Soundings

Seven times into the wind she flings the age-old query
Why am I?

Six questions boomerang
off the edge of sky
return six fathoms of silence
the cold of tarnished silver.

The seventh question
nicks the skin of God.
A drop of omniscience
splashes her cheek

steadies in-filling, out-breathing
the rhythm of her lungs
fortifies her walk, bed to bath to kitchen to car to work
warms, finally, her hands and feet.

She feels her full sixty-six inches, more substantial than water
able now to render echo.

Reprisal

on breath of day
full summer
you left me

alone
I beat the sky
to wound

the space you filled
a cold rises from deep
within, so cold it burns

in this wintry
white heat
I leave you

My Breath Is Red

root chakra

Red is longing, and my skin aches.
The base of my spine is plateau
the top ledge of a cube anchored
with roots spiralling deep
into the earth, into molten chaos.
I listen for red
invite its suffusion. Heat
rises, fills my feet and legs, propels
me to dance, then carry myself tall.

Blue

throat chakra

I am blue, the fifth floor of a seven-tiered tower.
To step past my doorway, you must be prepared
to be drenched, for I am oceans of blue.
I will cover your shoes, ride your shins, splash

all over you. When you enter willingly
there is nothing you cannot say.
The waterfall in the corner
is perpetual permission; come
walk beneath me. Dip a brush
into my depths and paint canvas.
Open your mouth and sing
Mozart, or Purcell. Strum a guitar
a violin, a harp. Or shape phrases
on a blank page. Choose,
let blue flow through.

When There Is Space for Breath

I have never seen her like this.
Talking fast, her eyes narrow, her whole body vibrating.
So exhausted that her back, which never gives her trouble
has seized.

On the massage table, her breath is tight.
There's a weight on my chest, she says. *It's fear. I'm afraid*
my heart will break.
I clear the energy at her collarbones, her neck
then hold her head, imagine for her a free passage for air.

Oh! There's a hawk rising
out of my chest! It's hovering above me
peering into my eyes.
I am the hawk, she says, *and yet*
it is still above me.

Her breath is free now, more full.
The weight gone. Her eyes are soft
unguarded, sure. *I've had an owl as a guide, but never*
a hawk, she said. *It's here to offer a new panorama.*
Her stride out the door is steady, eager.

Green Infinity

You think it's plasticine, formed
by a child's hand into an asymmetrical cone
a seven layered spiral. The fourth level fat and wide
the top spindly, not quite sealing itself. It sits
leans to one side, challenges

your perceptions. For it is not plasticine,
not a green snake wrapped round and round itself
but paint, thick, coiled, and dried. A vessel to hold
your dreams. No better colour to unfold the world.

When you hold the cone to your nose, you catch
a whiff of ancient wisdom. Sniff deeply
and take care. Though you can hold
this spiral in the palm of your hand
don't squeeze too hard, for its lungs
like yours
are fragile.

Dancing in Circles

I have travelled this maze since dawn
thinking I knew my way
thinking I understood why you left.
These winding paths were never for you; not for you
spirals that could go out of control.
You would take squares and build a careful house
pack it with straight things, line it
with certainties. When I find my way
out of here I will dance in circles
without you.

Green

mist circles me in

the hills are resplendent in fresh growth
trees shimmer like lace
life pushing death aside
fiddleheads unfurling

green, the taste of rain in the labyrinth of letting go
the scent of unfettered conversation
the tickle in veins
bubbles upsurging from glacier runoff

green, the colour of yes

Radical Surgery

It's not normal to line up yogurt containers and pails
on your window ledge to catch dripping water, to empty them
several times each day, sometimes hourly.
To pull down one section of drywall and end up gutted
to the studs. Joists and headers should not be black with rot.
You're not supposed to see the underside of shingles
from inside your house. And.
Wasp nests. Do. Not. Belong. In your rafters.
          It's the way of renovation plans. It's necessary. Get rid
of the skylights, the leaking windows.
Excise the rotten joists and headers. Tear off shingles
the sheathing, hell, the whole kitchen roof, the door, because
sometimes you have to start from scratch.

But when the work day ends and the roof still has a gaping hole
and it looks like rain it means
climbing up and tacking down a tarp in the fading light;
it means scrambling because the roofer will be here tomorrow
not next week like he first thought; it means savaging, not
salvaging, a section of siding because the sheathing underneath
is rotten and the power person is here to replace the meter
and we must do it NOW before he can do his part.

And when there's time to step back and take stock,
there it is, a rebuilt addition. The diseased portion carved away
the bones naked but safe, clean, strong.
Time to dress it up.

The Drum

The sound pulses over the hill
spreads through the valley
like mist rising above a lake.
A pause longer than seems right.
The thrum begins again, steady and strong, owning everything
to anchor my feet, pierce
my soles and seep into my circling
blood until my heart is its beat
until my breath is gone
until its skin and mine are one.

Acknowledgements

Thanks to the Saskatchewan Writers' Guild for their Apprenticeship Program, and to my mentor Barbara Klar who first inspired me to think of my collection of poems as a manuscript. Your wise teaching showed me the way forward. Thanks to Sue Cason, Margi Hollingshead, Elspeth Mackenzie, and Andrew Quackenbush for reading the entire manuscript and offering insight into its overarching themes. I am deeply grateful to my sister, Gail Fitzpatrick, whose financial generosity allowed me to take time from work to focus on this writing.

I would not have completed this project without the consistent writing support and encouragement of Donalda Jones, Karen Wallace, and Morgan Traquair. Thank you for believing in me, and for envisioning with me the end product of a book.

Thanks as well to Thistledown Press for making my dream come true. And special thanks, Michael Kenyon, for being such a generous and insightful editor. You helped make my poems shine, and I am most grateful.

I am ever thankful for my partner Elspeth, she of the sweet Scottish neck, who has companioned me daily. Your cheerleading has kept me going. You rock!

"Fragments from Hubble" and "Regret" appeared in *Spring* 2017, and "Why I Want to Travel the Stars" appeared in *The Society* 2018.